A GUIDE TO

TWELFTH NIGHT

The Shakespeare Handbooks

Guides available now:

- Antony & Cleopatra
- As You Like It
- Hamlet
- Henry IV, Part 1
- Julius Caesar
- King Lear
- Macbeth
- A Midsummer Night's Dream
- Romeo & Juliet
- The Tempest
- Twelfth Night

Further titles in preparation.

The Shakespeare Handbooks

A Guide to
Twelfth Night

by Alistair McCallum

Upstart Crow Publications

First published in 1996 by
Upstart Crow Publications

Reprinted 2004, 2009 and 2017

Copyright © Alistair McCallum 1996

A CIP catalogue record for this book
is available from the British Library

ISBN 978 1 899747 01 6

Printed in Great Britain by Print2demand Ltd,
17 Burgess Road, Ivyhouse Lane, Hastings,
East Sussex TN35 4NR

www.shakespeare-handbooks.com

Setting the scene

Shakespeare wrote *Twelfth Night* in or around 1601. He was in his mid-thirties, a successful dramatist and actor, and a member – and shareholder – of the most prestigious theatre company in London.

Right from the start, *Twelfth Night* seems to have been a great success with audiences. The notebook of a young lawyer, written in 1602 and still in existence, records how much he enjoyed a performance of the play, which had been staged at his law school by Shakespeare's company. The play was chosen a number of times by King James I's Master of the Revels for performance at the royal court.

Fifty years after Shakespeare's death, when Shakespearean comedy was generally unfashionable, *Twelfth Night* remained popular, mainly in the form of adaptations – frequently set to music – by other authors. By 1750, Shakespeare's own play, rather than these reworked versions, was established again as a favourite, and has remained so ever since.

Twelfth Night, with its lyrical poetry, its boisterous humour and its deep seriousness, is regarded by many as representing the peak of Shakespeare's achievement in comedy. The play is often linked to *Much Ado About Nothing* and *As You Like It*, the other great comedies from this period in Shakespeare's life; the three are often referred to as the 'mature' comedies, or sometimes as the 'romantic' or 'festive' comedies. *Twelfth Night* is the last and most profound of the three.

Although Shakespeare continued to write comedies after *Twelfth Night*, these were much darker and more problematic works, and his attention was increasingly turning to tragedy. *Hamlet* was already under way, and the other great tragedies were to follow over the next few years.

"If the light playing on As You Like It *is that of the morning sun, the sun in* Twelfth Night *is now mellower and later, afternoon sunshine with a hint of sunset in its quality ... in the distance we hear the sadder notes underlying the romantic ... the golden moment passed, and Shakespeare was not to write this kind of play again."*

David Daiches, *A Critical History of English Literature*

Unrequited love, grief …

Orsino, Duke of Illyria, is hopelessly in love with the Countess Olivia.

She, however, has no interest in him or his feelings; her brother died recently, and she wishes to be left alone, to mourn him in total seclusion.

… and calamity at sea

Off the coast of Illyria, a ship has been torn apart in a storm. Among the passengers were two twins, Viola and Sebastian.

There have been few survivors.

Curtain up

A true romantic

Duke Orsino is preoccupied with love. His passion for Olivia is all he can think of, and its intensity is almost unbearable. He is restless and dissatisfied, but at the same time is enjoying the sense of vitality that comes with being in love.

Music is playing, and Orsino is listening intently. He wants the music to sweep over him and soothe the hungry yearning of his love for Olivia:

> *Duke:* If music be the food of love, play on,
> Give me excess of it, that, surfeiting,[1]
> The appetite may sicken, and so die.
> That strain again, it had a dying fall:
> O, it came o'er my ear like the sweet sound
> That breathes upon a bank of violets,
> Stealing and giving odour.
>
> [1] *over-indulging*

The music continues, Orsino luxuriating in its sweetness and sadness.

But Orsino quickly tires of the music. Love is so powerful, he muses, that it swallows up all other experiences and soon renders them worthless; being in love means being condemned to a state of continual craving.

When a courtier tries to distract him, it only serves to remind him of his own plight:

Curio: Will you go hunt, my lord?
Duke: What, Curio?
Curio: The hart.
Duke: Why so I do, the noblest that I have.
          O, when mine eyes did see Olivia first,
          Methought she purg'd [1] the air of pestilence;
          That instant was I turned into a hart,
          And my desires, like fell [2] and cruel hounds,
          E'er since pursue me.

[1] *cleansed, purified*
[2] *fierce, terrible*

> *"From the very first lines everything in* Twelfth Night *is ambiguous. The hunt is for Olivia. But the hunter has been hunted down himself."*
>
> Jan Kott, *Shakespeare Our Contemporary*, 1965

In January 1601, Shakespeare's company of players – the Chamberlain's Men – was commissioned to put on a play for Queen Elizabeth I and her guest of honour, a 28-year-old Italian Duke. It is not known which play was performed, but it is likely to have been one of Shakespeare's: the Duke's own description of the play, which he mentioned approvingly in a letter to his wife, suggests it may have been *Much Ado About Nothing*.

Shakespeare would almost certainly have acted in the play, and seen – and perhaps met – the young Duke, who cut a gallant, attractive figure in the Queen's court. For whatever reason, it seems that Shakespeare chose to borrow the name of the guest – Duke Virginio Orsino of Bracciano – for the romantic ruler of Illyria in *Twelfth Night*, the play he was to complete later in the year.

Olivia is resolute

A messenger sent by Orsino to Olivia returns. He was not even allowed to speak to her, he tells Orsino. She is still mourning her brother, and has resolved to cut herself off from the outside world for seven years:

Valentine: … like a cloistress[1] she will veiled walk,
And water once a day her chamber round
With eye-offending brine: all this to season[2]
A brother's dead love, which she would keep fresh
And lasting, in her sad remembrance.

[1] *nun*
[2] *preserve*

Orsino is not discouraged by the news; in fact, it only convinces him of her true, loving nature, and makes him all the more eager to win her heart.

His spirits raised, the Duke leaves, keen to carry on revelling in the pleasures of love. This time it will be nature, rather than music, which provides the setting:

> *Duke:* Away before me to sweet beds of flowers!
> Love-thoughts lie rich when canopied with bowers.

Viola's sea-voyage is cut short — I, ii

A few survivors from a shipwreck have managed to reach the shores of Illyria. Among them are the vessel's captain and Viola. The fate of Viola's twin brother Sebastian is unknown: he had tied himself to a piece of wreckage which, when last seen, was floating out at sea.

The captain, who knows Illyria, tells Viola about Orsino, his love for Olivia, and her mourning and desire for solitude. Olivia's situation strikes a chord with Viola; the idea of withdrawing from the outside world to come to terms with the sudden, drastic change in her life appeals to her. She even thinks of trying to join Olivia's household. However, as the captain points out, Olivia does not want company. Instead, Viola decides to get to know Duke Orsino. She asks the captain to help her gain entry into Orsino's court. She wants him to accompany her and provide her with a disguise:

> *Viola:* I prithee (and I'll pay thee bounteously)
> Conceal me what I am, and be my aid
> For such disguise as haply shall become
> The form of my intent. I'll serve this duke ...

The captain agrees to go along with her plan, and they set off for Duke Orsino's court.

Disorder in Olivia's household

Sir Toby Belch, Olivia's uncle, does not share the general sympathy with her bereavement.

> *Sir Toby:* What a plague means my niece to take the death of her brother thus? I am sure care's an enemy to life.

Maria, Olivia's maidservant, scolds Sir Toby for his noisy, drunken revelry, which frequently continues into the small hours, much to Olivia's annoyance. He is at his worst, says Maria, in the company of a certain knight, Sir Andrew Aguecheek, who – with Sir Toby's encouragement – is keen to marry Olivia.

Sir Toby is unrepentant. Sir Andrew, he assures Maria, is wealthy, valiant and cultured; and when they drink, it is to the health of his niece Olivia.

> *Sir Toby:* … I'll drink to her as long as there is a passage in my throat, and drink in Illyria: he's a coward and a coistrel[1] that will not drink to my niece till his brains turn o' th' toe, like a parish top.

> [1] *knave*

"… a man once drunk with wine or strong drink rather resembleth a brute than a Christian man. For do not his eyes begin to stare and to be red, fiery and bleared … Doth he not froth and foam at the mouth like a boar? Are not his wits and spirits, as it were, drowned? Is not his understanding altogether decayed? … The drunkard, in his drunkenness, killeth his friend, revileth his lover, discloseth secrets, and regardeth no man."

Philip Stubbes, *The Anatomie of Abuses*, 1583

Sir Andrew now arrives. He does not live up to Sir Toby's description. As soon as he meets Maria, his tenuous grasp of the English language becomes obvious:

Sir Andrew: Bless you, fair shrew.
Maria: And you too, sir.
Sir Toby: Accost, Sir Andrew, accost.
Sir Andrew: What's that?
Sir Toby: My niece's chambermaid.
Sir Andrew: Good mistress Accost, I desire better acquaintance...
Sir Toby: ... You mistake, knight. 'Accost' is front her, board her, woo her, assail her.
Sir Andrew: By my troth, I would not undertake her in this company. Is that the meaning of 'accost'?

Maria, whose opinion of Sir Andrew as a slow-witted ignoramus is quickly confirmed, takes her leave.

Sir Toby delights in teasing Sir Andrew and taking advantage of his obtuseness. In one brief but gruesome image, he pictures Sir Andrew with a prostitute, trapped in the works of an unstoppable sexual machine, being operated relentlessly like a spinning wheel, his lank hair falling out from exhaustion and disease in the process:

Sir Andrew: I would I had bestowed that time in the tongues that I have in fencing, dancing and bear-baiting. O, had I but followed the arts!
Sir Toby: Then hadst thou had an excellent head of hair.
Sir Andrew: Why, would that have mended my hair?
Sir Toby: Past question, for thou seest it will not curl by nature.
Sir Andrew: But it becomes me well enough, does't not?
Sir Toby: Excellent, it hangs like flax on a distaff; and I hope to see a housewife take thee between her legs, and spin it off.

Sir Andrew is unsure of his chances with Olivia, and is inclined to go home. However, he is quickly persuaded to stay, and, egged on by Sir Toby, joins him in his drunken revelry.

Cesario is sent on a mission

Viola has disguised herself as a man, and, calling herself Cesario, has managed to get into Duke Orsino's court. The Duke has taken to the young newcomer at once, finding him a sensitive and trustworthy companion.

Orsino has a job for Cesario. He wants the youth to gain access to Olivia, refusing to take no for an answer, and spell out how much Orsino is in love with her. Orsino urges Cesario to make the declaration as theatrical as possible; he may succeed where others have failed.

> *Duke:*   ... unfold the passion of my love,
> Surprise her with discourse of my dear faith;
> It shall become thee well to act my woes:
> She will attend it better in thy youth,
> Than in a nuncio's[1] of more grave aspect.
>
> [1] *messenger*

Cesario agrees to do his best. But beneath the disguise, Viola finds herself in an agonising situation: she must go to Olivia to declare Orsino's love, but she herself has fallen in love with Orsino.

> *Viola:*   ... yet, a barful strife![1]
> Whoe'er I woo, myself would be his wife.
>
> [1] *a conflict that makes the task difficult*

She sets off, reluctantly, for Olivia's house.

An 'allowed fool'

Feste is the jester of Olivia's household, at liberty to comment on anyone and anything. He has been away for a long time – he tends to wander freely from place to place – and Maria is scolding him for his long absence.

As they argue, Olivia enters. She is accompanied by Malvolio, the dour senior steward of her household. As Maria predicted, Olivia is displeased with Feste: however, he soon manages to work his way back into her favour.

The character of Feste is not just a theatrical invention. The old tradition of keeping fools was very much alive in Shakespeare's day. The fool – often someone with a physical or mental disability – was expected to be a continual source of entertainment, and was allowed to make fun of anyone, regardless of status. Fools were not only kept for amusement: they were also believed to ward off evil spirits and bring good luck.

Fools were employed in establishments of all sorts, ranging from the court of Queen Elizabeth I to private households, taverns and brothels. The tradition did not die out until well into the 18th century.

Although his mistress is fond of the fool, Malvolio does not have a good word to say about him. He disapproves both of fools and of people who laugh at them. As far as he is concerned, foolery is no more than childish attention-seeking, and Feste does not deserve the interest he arouses:

> *Malvolio:* I marvel your ladyship takes delight in such a barren rascal: I saw him put down the other day with an ordinary fool,[1] that has no more brain than a stone. Look you now, he's out of his guard already: unless you laugh and minister occasion to him, he is gagged.
>
> [1] *tavern comedian*

Olivia observes that it is Malvolio, not the fool, who is being self-centred. He would do well, she advises him, not to take everything so personally:

> *Olivia:* O, you are sick of self-love, Malvolio, and taste with a distempered appetite. To be generous, guiltless, and of free disposition, is to take those things for bird-bolts[1] that you deem cannon-bullets. There is no slander in an allowed fool ...
>
> [1] *blunt arrows*

Feste is delighted with Olivia's judgement.

Is Malvolio the only character who is 'sick of self-love'?

"... the same charge may be brought against both Olivia and Orsino, but the action is to show that while their sickness is curable, Malvolio's is not."

Stanley Wells, *Shakespeare: A Dramatic Life*, 1994

A visitor for Olivia

Maria brings news of a young gentleman at the gate. Olivia sends Malvolio to deal with him: if he is another messenger from Orsino, Malvolio is to invent some excuse or other to get rid of him.

Sir Toby, who has been talking to the visitor, wanders in drunkenly: but Olivia cannot get any sense out of him. He staggers out again, and Feste is sent out to look after him.

Malvolio returns. The visitor, he tells Olivia, insists on seeing her, and refuses to accept any excuses. Malvolio is baffled by the visitor's assertiveness, but struck by his youthful appearance:

> *Malvolio:* 'Tis with him in standing water,[1] between boy and man. He is very well-favoured, and he speaks very shrewishly. One would think his mother's milk were scarce out of him.
>
> [1] *at the turn of the tide*

Olivia's curiosity is aroused, and she decides to allow the young man in. Before he comes in, she covers her face with her mourning veil.

Cesario makes an impression

The visitor is Cesario – Viola in her male disguise – who has been sent by Orsino. Cesario starts by asking pointedly which of the present company is the lady of the house. When this is established, he launches into his speech with a distinct lack of ceremony:

> *Viola:*   Most radiant, exquisite, and unmatchable beauty –
> I pray you tell me if this be the lady of the house,
> for I never saw her. I would be loath to cast away
> my speech: for besides that it is excellently well
> penned, I have taken great pains to con it.[1]
>
> [1] *learn it by heart*

Olivia is puzzled by the young stranger who is so determined to wade through his prepared speech, and she starts to become impatient with him. Undeterred, Cesario assures Olivia that he will come to the point, and tells her he would rather speak to her on her own.

> *Viola:*   It alone concerns your ear … I hold the olive in my
> hand: my words are as full of peace, as matter.
> *Olivia:* Yet you began rudely. What are you? What would you?
> *Viola:*   The rudeness that hath appeared in me have I
> learned from my entertainment.

Olivia is amused by Cesario's self-assurance, and she tells her attendants to leave them on their own. She relaxes and draws back her veil, and they talk of Orsino. She assures Cesario that, although she respects Orsino, she does not love him.

16

As they talk, Olivia finds herself more and more attracted to the young messenger, even though he accuses her of pride and cruelty. When Cesario takes his leave, Olivia hints that he might come back another time to tell her how Orsino has taken her rejection.

As soon as Cesario has gone, Olivia realises that she is falling in love with him:

Olivia: How now?
         Even so quickly may one catch the plague?
         Methinks I feel this youth's perfections
         With an invisible and subtle stealth
         To creep in at mine eyes. Well, let it be.

She decides immediately that she must see him again.

Even so quickly may one catch the plague?

The plague is mentioned a few times in *Twelfth Night*. Outbreaks of bubonic plague were a regular occurrence in England, and particularly in London, at the time.

When a severe epidemic occurred in London – defined as more than 30 deaths a week – the theatres were closed down by the authorities who believed, probably correctly, that large public assemblies helped to spread the disease. Unfortunately for the theatres, epidemics tended to happen during the summer, when the theatres – which had no lighting or heating – did most of their business.

At the time of *Twelfth Night*, there had not been a major epidemic for several years. The plague was far from over, however, and was to afflict the London theatres throughout Shakespeare's career. References to the plague are fairly light-hearted in *Twelfth Night*; in later plays, any mentions of the disease tend to be more sombre and menacing.

Olivia suddenly comes up with an idea. Calling Malvolio, she gives him a ring to take to Cesario. He left it behind, she explains, despite her protestations: Malvolio is to take it back to him. At the same time, he should instruct Cesario to come back tomorrow.

She hardly knows what she is doing, and is shocked at this sudden impulsiveness in herself. The only solution is to put herself in the hands of destiny and hope for the best:

> *Olivia:* Fate, show thy force; ourselves we do not owe.[1]
> What is decreed, must be: and be this so.
>
> [1] *own, take responsibility for*

Another survivor from the shipwreck   II, i

Sebastian, Viola's twin brother, is alive and well. He was rescued from the sea by Antonio, a seafarer living in Illyria, at whose house he has been recovering.

Sebastian believes that his sister died in the storm. He now wants to be alone with his grief, and is leaving Antonio's house. Antonio has become very attached to his new friend, and is unwilling that they should part company: but Sebastian insists, graciously but firmly, that he must go.

As Sebastian leaves, he mentions that his destination is Orsino's court. Antonio, who has enemies at the court, is taken aback. Then, on an impulse, he decides to follow his friend secretly:

> *Antonio:* But come what may, I do adore thee so,
> That danger shall seem sport, and I will go.

The truth dawns on Viola

Malvolio catches up with Cesario. He gives back the ring which – he has been led to believe – Cesario forced on Olivia. Cesario refuses to take the ring: Malvolio throws it on the ground in front of him, and departs.

Left alone, Viola puzzles over the ring. She soon realises what has happened, and is dismayed at the confusion that has resulted from her disguise. She cannot see a way out of her predicament: all she can do, she decides, is let events take their own course.

> *Viola:*
>   As I am man,
> My state is desperate[1] for my master's love:
> As I am woman (now alas the day!)
> What thriftless sighs shall poor Olivia breathe?
> O time, thou must untangle this, not I,
> It is too hard a knot for me t'untie.
>
> [1] *hopeless*

Sir Toby's revelry is interrupted

Sir Toby and Sir Andrew are enjoying another night of drunkenness. Feste joins them and, with a little persuasion and a couple of coins from the others, sings a song. The song is of love and youth, of the uncertainty of the future and the importance of the present:

> What is love? 'Tis not hereafter,
> Present mirth hath present laughter:
>   What's to come is still unsure.
> In delay there lies no plenty,
> Then come and kiss me, sweet and twenty:
>   Youth's a stuff will not endure.

Sir Toby and Sir Andrew are delighted, and eventually all three join together in a rowdy chorus. Maria charges in and tries, unsuccessfully, to quieten them down.

Shortly Malvolio too comes to investigate the noise. He reprimands them at length, singling out Sir Toby for particular criticism. His main fault, says Malvolio, is to have upset the Countess Olivia:

> *Malvolio:* ... though she harbours you as her kinsman, she's nothing allied to[1] your disorders. If you can separate yourself and your misdemeanours, you are welcome to the house: if not ... she is very willing to bid you farewell.
>
> [1] *will not tolerate*

Sir Toby carries on singing. He cannot bear Malvolio, whom he considers self-important and puritanical:

> *Sir Toby:* Art any more than a steward? Dost thou think because thou art virtuous, there shall be no more cakes and ale?

Malvolio does not attempt to argue with the drunken Sir Toby. He reproves Maria for supplying the drink which fuels this late-night rowdiness; Olivia will get to hear of it. Malvolio makes a dignified exit.

Dost thou think because thou art virtuous, there shall be no more cakes and ale?

"This most famous sentence in the play is more than Sir Toby disposing of his niece's steward; it is the old world resisting the new, it is the life of hiccups and melancholy trying to ignore latter-day puritanism and efficiency."

Mark Van Doren, *Shakespeare*, 1939

A conspiracy against Malvolio

A mood of resentment descends on the company, and they are determined to get their own back on Malvolio. Maria tells the others to be patient and calm for the moment; since Cesario's visit, Olivia has been unusually agitated, and is very sensitive to disturbance of any kind.

Maria has a plan to make a fool of Malvolio. She has always disliked him, not for his puritanism – he is not as pious as he seems – but for his insincerity and his high opinion of himself.

> *Maria:* The devil a Puritan that he is, or anything
> constantly, but a time-pleaser,[1] an affectioned ass,
> that cons state without book[2] ... the best persuaded
> of himself, so crammed (as he thinks) with
> excellencies, that it is his grounds of faith that all
> that look on him love him: and on that vice in him
> will my revenge find notable cause to work.
>
> [1] *one who changes opinions to suit his situation*
> [2] *memorises phrases that sound dignified and stately*

Maria, whose handwriting is very similar to her lady's, plans to forge a love-letter from Olivia to Malvolio. She is convinced that Malvolio will be taken in, and intends to plant the others where they can observe his reactions.

There is nothing specific in the play to suggest that it takes place at the time of Twelfth Night (the night of January 5th, leading to Epiphany on January 6th). However, the nature of the occasion may be significant; Twelfth Night was traditionally a night of unruliness and feasting, but at the same time it marks the end of the festive season. The play is undoubtedly darker, more questioning and more uncertain than Shakespeare's previous comedies.

"Twelfth night is here, and soon we shall be unpinning the decorations and facing bleak reality. Already there is a sharp nipping air blowing from the tragedies ..."

John Wain, *The Living World of Shakespeare*, 1964

Financial considerations

Maria goes off to bed, delighted with her scheme. Sir Toby bids her a fond goodnight: she's a fine woman, he tells Sir Andrew, and, what's more, she loves him dearly. Then Sir Toby bluntly brings up the subject of money. Sir Andrew, it turns out, has been supplying him with money in the expectation that Sir Toby will be able to arrange his marriage to the Countess. Sir Toby now needs more.

Sir Toby: Thou hadst need send for more money.
Sir Andrew: If I cannot recover your niece, I am a foul way out.[1]
Sir Toby: Send for money, knight; if thou hast her not i' th' end, call me cut.[2]

> [1] *in a terrible mess*
> [2] *a horse that has been docked: or one that has been castrated*

Sir Andrew, as usual, is easily persuaded. Sir Toby declares that it is too late to go to bed now; they may as well carry on drinking.

Orsino is still enthralled by love

News of Olivia's rejection has not deterred Orsino. He is as much in love, and as keen to talk about it, as ever. In his state, he explains to Cesario, it is impossible to concentrate for long on anything other than his beloved.

Cesario's sympathy with his feelings arouses Orsino's curiosity; is he, like his master, in love?

Duke:	My life upon't, young though thou art, thine eye
	Hath stay'd upon some favour that it loves.
	Hath it not, boy?
Viola:	A little, by your favour.
Duke:	What kind of woman is't?
Viola:	Of your complexion.
Duke:	She is not worth thee then. What years, i' faith?
Viola:	About your years, my lord.
Duke:	Too old, by heaven!

He should find a woman younger than himself, advises Orsino; a man's feelings are changeable, and he needs a younger woman to keep him stable and faithful.

Orsino calls for music and singing. His taste is for traditional, simple, romantic ballads, and he asks for Feste to be brought in. The jester arrives, and obliges with a song about a lover who wishes to die rather than face life without his beloved:

Feste:	Come away,[1] come away death,
	And in sad cypress let me be laid.
	Fie away, fie away breath,
	I am slain by a fair cruel maid …

[1] *hurry to me*

Orsino is delighted with the sad song.

Cesario speaks up for women

Orsino instructs Cesario to go to Olivia again and persuade her of his love. He brushes aside the boy's suggestion that Olivia may not love him.

Cesario persists: surely it is possible for love to be unrequited? If a woman loved Orsino as he loves Olivia, for example, then she would have to face the fact that her love would not be returned.

Orsino is amused at the idea that a woman's love could be likened to his own overwhelming passion. A woman's love, he explains to Cesario, is shallow and weak in comparison.

In her eagerness to contradict Orsino's dismissive view of women's emotions, Viola nearly gives herself away. However, she manages to contain herself, and tries to persuade Orsino with an example:

> *Viola:* My father had a daughter lov'd a man,
> As it might be perhaps, were I a woman,
> I should your lordship.
> *Duke:* And what's her history?
> *Viola:* A blank, my lord: she never told her love,
> But let concealment like a worm i' th' bud
> Feed on her damask cheek: she pin'd in thought,
> And with a green and yellow[1] melancholy
> She sat like Patience on a monument,
> Smiling at grief. Was not this love indeed?
> We men may say more, swear more, but indeed
> Our shows are more than will: for still we prove
> Much in our vows, but little in our love.
>
> [1] *pale, sickly*

Orsino is moved, and wishes to know what happened to Cesario's sister. Viola's enigmatic answer hints both at her own identity and at the supposed death of her brother:

Duke: But died thy sister of her love, my boy?
Viola: I am all the daughters of my father's house,
And all the brothers too: and yet I know not.

The meaning of the riddle escapes Orsino, and Cesario hurries off on his mission.

---

*... She sat like Patience on a monument,
Smiling at grief.*

"Viola's parable ... creates a temporary suspension of the flow of time in the play as she looks backward to an imagined past which is at the same time an image of the future that she fears for herself ..."

Stanley Wells, *Shakespeare: A Dramatic Life*, 1994

Malvolio's daydreams revealed

Sir Toby, Sir Andrew and Fabian, another member of Olivia's household, are in the garden waiting to see the results of Maria's deception.

Maria arrives, and tells them to hide in a box-tree and keep quiet: Malvolio is on his way. Maria drops the forged letter where he will see it, and makes a hasty exit.

Malvolio enters. Spurred on by a few well-chosen words from Maria, he is already indulging in his favourite fantasy of being married to Countess Olivia:

> *Malvolio:* Maria once told me she did affect me,[1] and I have
> heard herself come thus near, that should she fancy,[2]
> it should be one of my complexion. Besides, she
> uses me with a more exalted respect than any one
> else that follows her ... To be Count Malvolio!
>
> [1] *was fond of me*
> [2] *fall in love*

The three men in the box-tree, overcome by turns with hilarity, contempt and rage, can hardly control themselves.

Malvolio's fantasy includes the pleasures of power and social status as well as those of love. He imagines himself giving his kinsman Toby – no longer Sir – a friendly but serious lecture on his drinking and his unsuitable company.

Sir Toby is furious, while Sir Andrew, correctly guessing that he is the unsuitable company in question, is pleased at his own astuteness.

Malvolio is taken in

At this point Malvolio comes across the letter left by Maria. He recognises the handwriting as Olivia's, and opens the letter anxiously.

The letter starts with a poem declaring the writer's feelings. She complains that her love, and the object of her love, must remain secret:

> Jove knows I love;
> But who?
> Lips, do not move,
> No man must know.

Malvolio is agitated, realising that his own name could neatly fit into this verse. He reads on. The last line of the poem is enigmatic:

> ... M.O.A.I. doth sway[1] my life.
>
> > [1] *dominate, govern*

He ponders the four initials. Although he cannot fully decipher them, he decides, with growing excitement, that they could easily represent his name. The letter continues:

> In my stars I am above thee, but be not afraid
> of greatness. Some are born great, some achieve
> greatness, and some have greatness thrust upon 'em.

The writer advises Malvolio to prepare himself for the social status that he is about to acquire:

> Be opposite[1] with a kinsman, surly with servants ...
> put thyself into the trick of singularity[2] ... Go to,
> thou art made, if thou desir'st to be so. If not, let me
> see thee a steward still, the fellow of servants ...
>
> > [1] *argumentative*
> > [2] *individuality, unconventionality*

The writer lets him know how attractive she finds him in yellow, cross-gartered stockings: finally, she urges him to smile as much as possible in her presence.

Malvolio is overjoyed. There is no doubt in his mind that the love-letter was written by Countess Olivia and intended for him. He resolves to do exactly as the letter tells him: he will be disdainful, rude and eccentric, and he will wear cross-gartered yellow stockings. As he leaves, he is already practising his smiles.

The onlookers are ecstatic to see that the trick has succeeded. Maria returns, and assures them that Malvolio's performance in front of Olivia will be worth seeing. The clothes he intends to wear are precisely those that Olivia hates, and in her present state of anxiety and confusion a grinning Malvolio will be more than she can bear.

A disappointment for Olivia   III, i

On Duke Orsino's instructions, Cesario has come to Olivia's house again. In the garden, he comes across the fool, who was singing at Orsino's court not long ago. Feste explains that he is a great wanderer:

> *Feste:* Foolery, sir, does walk about the orb like the sun,
> it shines everywhere. I would be sorry, sir, but[1] the
> fool should be as oft with your master as with my
> mistress ...
>
> [1] *I would be disappointed if it were not true*

Feste goes off to tell Olivia of the caller. The two knights come out, followed by Olivia herself. Sir Andrew is impressed by Cesario's elegant greeting of Olivia, and makes a mental note of his phrases for future reference. Olivia asks to be left alone with the visitor.

Cesario dutifully starts to remind Olivia of Orsino's love for her, but she is not interested;

Olivia: ... But would you undertake another suit,
I had rather hear you to solicit that,
Than music from the spheres.[1]

[1] *music generated by the revolving of the heavens, inaudible to mortals*

Olivia apologises profusely for her deception in sending the ring to Cesario. However, now that it is done, her feelings have been made plain, and she is defenceless. She is desperate to hear that her love is returned, but it is not to be: Cesario tells her, gently, that he sympathises with her but does not love her.

Olivia perseveres

At first, Olivia accepts the bad news stoically. As she reflects on her brief experience of intense passion, the clock strikes, and she is brought back down to earth. She tells Cesario that she envies the woman he will eventually marry:

Olivia: ... I will not have you,
And yet when wit and youth is come to harvest,
Your wife is like to reap a proper man.

Cesario establishes that Olivia has nothing to say to Orsino, and is about to leave. Olivia makes a final, desperate declaration of her love:

Olivia: I love thee so, that maugre all thy pride,[1]
Nor wit nor reason can my passion hide.
... Love sought is good, but given unsought is better.

[1] *despite your indifference*

But it is to no avail. Cesario assures her firmly that he does not, cannot and will not love her. As he goes, she appeals to him to visit again, even if it is only on Orsino's behalf.

> *"Shakespeare's way in the great scenes is to involve us deeply, by packing our minds with private awarenesses that confer a sense of personal responsibility toward the action."*
>
> Bertrand Evans, *Shakespeare's Comedies*, 1960

Sir Andrew decides to confront his rival   III, ii

Sir Andrew may be slow-witted, but the attention that Olivia has been paying to the young Cesario has not escaped his notice. He intends to leave, and give up his hopes of marrying the Countess.

His companions immediately try to dissuade him. Olivia is only favouring Cesario in order to make Sir Andrew jealous, explains Fabian; this is a sign of her love. She wants to provoke a reaction from Sir Andrew, but none has been forthcoming.

> *Fabian:* She did show favour to the youth in your sight
> only to exasperate you, to awake your dormouse
> valour ... You should then have accosted her, and
> with some excellent jests, fire-new from the mint,
> you should have banged the youth into dumbness.
> This was looked for at your hand, and this was
> balked[1] ... you are now sailed into the north of my
> lady's opinion, where you will hang like an icicle
> on a Dutchman's beard, unless you do redeem it by
> some laudable attempt, either of valour or policy.[2]
>
> [1] *left undone*
> [2] *cunning strategy*

There is only one thing to do, Sir Toby advises him: he must challenge the young Cesario to a duel. Sir Andrew's success as a swordsman would be guaranteed to win Olivia over.

There is no time to lose, they assure Sir Andrew. He must write a fierce, scornful letter to Cesario, and Sir Toby will deliver it. Sir Andrew obediently goes off to compose his challenge.

Fabian remarks to Sir Toby that he seems to be able to manipulate Sir Andrew at will. Sir Toby agrees, boasting of the money that he has already conned out of him.

Maria comes in with news of Malvolio. The forged letter has worked; in order to please Olivia, he has dressed outlandishly, and

> *Maria:*   … he does smile his face into more lines than is in the new map with the augmentation of the Indies …

Sir Toby and Fabian are anxious to witness this spectacle, and Maria leads them off.

The 'new map' Maria mentions probably refers to a map of the world published in 1599, a couple of years before *Twelfth Night* was first performed. This map, which used the recently-devised Mercator Projection, showed the East Indies and the coast of New Holland (Australia) in more detail than ever before. The lines Maria has in mind are the rhumb lines, designed to help navigators establish their bearings, which criss-crossed the map in great numbers.

Maria's remark is a small reminder of the tremendous drive towards worldwide trade, exploration and colonisation that England, along with other European nations, was experiencing at the time.

Antonio catches up with Sebastian III, iii

Sebastian, Viola's twin brother, has left Antonio's house, where he had been recovering after his ordeal in the shipwreck. Antonio, unwilling to part company with his friend, secretly followed him, and has now caught up with him in the streets of the city.

Sebastian is curious about his new surroundings, and is keen to explore the city. However, Antonio cannot join him. They are not far from Orsino's court, and Antonio was once involved in a sea-battle against Orsino's forces. There was no bloodshed, he assures Sebastian; nevertheless, if the Duke's officers found him he would be in serious trouble.

Antonio sets off for an inn, the Elephant, to arrange their accommodation. Before he goes, he leaves his purse with Sebastian in case he wants to buy anything as he wanders around the city.

Malvolio is transformed III, iv

Olivia is torn by her feelings for Cesario. Despite his rejection, she cannot give up hope, and is determined to see him again. In her agitation she needs a calming influence, and calls for Malvolio:

> *Olivia:*   He is sad and civil,
> And suits well for a servant with my fortunes ...

Malvolio, who was already on his way to see her, arrives. Olivia is aghast at his ludicrous, playful behaviour, his gaudy yellow stockings with their cross-gartering, and his relentless smiling.

To Olivia's bewilderment, Malvolio starts to quote phrases from the forged love-letter. Olivia is distressed, fearing that he has suffered a sudden fit of madness.

A servant comes in to tell Olivia that he has managed, with difficulty, to persuade Cesario to visit again. Olivia hurries out to see him, urging the others to take good care of Malvolio.

Malvolio has deluded himself so completely that he fails to see Olivia's distress. As far as he is concerned, everything is going his way, and the Countess will soon be his. Sir Toby, Fabian and Maria all try to persuade him that he is possessed by the devil: but he treats them with contempt, just as the letter instructed him.

> *Malvolio:* Go hang yourselves all: you are idle, shallow
> things, I am not of your element: you shall know
> more hereafter.[1]

> [1] *later, when I am Count Malvolio*

Malvolio leaves. The others decide to pursue him and – using the excuse that he is a madman – imprison him in a dark room.

The words 'mad' and 'madness' crop up more frequently in *Twelfth Night* than in any other play by Shakespeare.

Ironically, no-one in the play is genuinely mad; any apparent madness is a result of deception, disguise or self-delusion.

Sir Andrew issues a challenge

Sir Andrew has finished working on his letter to Cesario, and proudly asks Sir Toby to read it. The letter is a hopeless tangle of absurd, incongruous threats and assertions:

> Youth, whatsoever thou art, thou art but a scurvy
> fellow. Wonder not, nor admire not in thy mind,
> why I do call thee so, for I will show thee no reason
> for't. Thou com'st to the Lady Olivia, and in my
> sight she uses thee kindly: but thou liest in thy
> throat; that is not the matter I challenge thee for.
> I will waylay thee going home, where if it be thy
> chance to kill me, thou kill'st me like a rogue and a
> villain …
> Thy friend, as thou usest him, and thy sworn enemy,
> Andrew Aguecheek.

The others congratulate Sir Andrew; his note is clever, brief, and bold, and is sure to provoke Cesario to a duel.

Sir Toby tells Sir Andrew to wait in a corner of the orchard, while he goes off to deliver the note to Cesario. He will then send the youth in Sir Andrew's direction, so the knight must prepare himself:

> *Sir Toby:* So soon as ever thou see'st him, draw, and as thou
> draw'st, swear horrible …

Sir Andrew goes off to the corner of the orchard, timidly asking if he can be excused from swearing.

Sir Toby realises that Cesario has too much sense to be frightened by Sir Andrew's inept attempt at a challenge. Instead of delivering the note, he will talk to the youth and convince him of Sir Andrew's anger and his ferocious reputation. When he brings the two of them together, each will be as petrified as the other:

> *Sir Toby:* This will so fright them both that they will kill one another by the look, like cockatrices.[1]
>
> [1] *legendary serpents that could kill with a glance*

He goes off to think of a suitably terrifying description of Sir Andrew to report to Cesario.

Olivia refuses to give up

Cesario has returned, reluctantly, to talk to Olivia. She admits to him that she has been rash in declaring her love so openly. However, her feelings are so powerful that she cannot deny them, and she refuses to feel ashamed. She gives Cesario a locket containing a miniature portrait of herself, and asks him to wear it.

Cesario continues to remind her that he has come on Orsino's behalf, but Olivia has by now lost interest in Orsino. It is Cesario she wants to see, and she asks him to come again tomorrow.

A warning for Cesario

As Olivia leaves, Sir Toby and Fabian rush in. Sir Toby wastes no time, launching into an urgent, detailed account of the danger that Cesario is in:

> *Sir Toby:* That defence thou hast, betake thee to't. Of what nature the wrongs are thou hast done him, I know not: but thy intercepter, full of despite, bloody as the hunter, attends thee at the orchard-end ... thy assailant is quick, skilful, and deadly.

Cesario is stunned. He cannot think of anyone who might have any reason to quarrel with him. Sir Toby assures him vigorously that this is the case, and paints a lurid picture of Sir Andrew:

> *Sir Toby:* ... if you hold your life at any price, betake you to your guard: for your opposite hath in him what youth, strength, skill, and wrath, can furnish man withal ... Souls and bodies hath he divorced three, and his incensement at this moment is so implacable that satisfaction can be none but by pangs of death and sepulchre.[1]
>
> [1] *the grave*

Cesario decides to go into the house, find Olivia and ask her to escort him away safely. But Sir Toby bars his way: the quarrel is on a point of honour, and if he will not face Sir Andrew, he must fight it out with Sir Toby himself.

Cesario asks Sir Toby to find out what he has done to upset the knight. Sir Toby agrees, and leaves him with Fabian.

Sir Andrew changes his mind

Fabian confirms to Cesario that everything Sir Toby says about his rival is true, even though his initial appearance may be misleading. He brings Cesario towards Sir Andrew, promising that he will do his best to placate the angry knight.

Meanwhile, Sir Andrew is waiting unhappily in the corner of the orchard. Sir Toby comes over and warns him that his opponent, Cesario, is a professional swordsman with a deadly reputation.

Sir Andrew's mind is immediately made up: he will abandon the contest. It is too late, says Sir Toby; his opponent is seething with rage, and Fabian is only just managing to restrain him at this very moment.

Sir Andrew, terror-stricken, begs Sir Toby to speak to the youth and offer him a gift if he will call off the duel. Sir Toby promises to do his best, and is secretly delighted with this unexpected bonus, which he has no intention of passing on to Cesario.

> *Sir Andrew:* Plague on't, and[1] I thought he had been valiant,
> and so cunning in fence, I'd have seen him damned
> ere I'd have challenged him. Let him let the matter
> slip, and I'll give him my horse, grey Capilet.
> *Sir Toby:* I'll make the motion.[2] Stand here, make a good
> show on't: this shall end without the perdition of
> souls. [*Aside*] Marry, I'll ride your horse as well as
> I ride you.
>
> [1] *if*
> [2] *propose the idea*

The duel commences …

Sir Toby returns to Cesario. Sir Andrew cannot go back on his word, he explains, and the duel must go ahead. However, he has calmed down considerably, and promises not to hurt the youth.

Sir Toby then delivers the same message to Sir Andrew:

> *Sir Toby:* Come, Sir Andrew, there's no remedy, the
> gentleman will for his honour's sake have one bout
> with you; he cannot by the duello[1] avoid it: but he
> has promised me, as he is a gentleman and a soldier,
> he will not hurt you. Come on, to't.
> *Sir Andrew:* Pray God he keep his oath!

> [1] *rules governing the conduct of duels*

Fabian and Sir Toby manage to drag the unwilling participants towards each other. Both trembling with fear, they draw their swords.

… and is interrupted

At this point, Antonio comes onto the scene. He lately parted company with Sebastian, lending him his purse.

In her male disguise as Cesario, Viola strongly resembles her twin brother, and Antonio takes her to be Sebastian. He is horrified to see that his young friend has got into a fight, and leaps to his defence:

> *Antonio:* Put up your sword! If this young gentleman
> Have done offence, I take the fault on me:
> If you offend him, I for him defy you.

Sir Toby, irritated by the intruder, draws his sword. He is about to take Antonio on when officers of the law rush in.

Antonio is arrested

Cesario and Sir Andrew, relieved that the duel has been interrupted, amicably put away their swords. Sir Andrew assures the puzzled Cesario that the offer of his horse still holds good:

> *Sir Andrew:* ... for that I promised you, I'll be as good as
> my word. He will bear you easily, and reins well.

The officers, recognising Antonio as a wanted man, guilty of piracy against the Duke, arrest him. Cesario, already in a state of confusion, is even more mystified when Antonio asks for the return of his purse. Cesario knows nothing about the purse, but offers to share what little money he has with the stranger.

Antonio, enraged that he has been cheated out of his purse, refuses. He publicly denounces his disloyal friend, whom he had recently saved from drowning:

> *Antonio:* This youth that you see here
> I snatch'd one half out of the jaws of death,
> Reliev'd[1] him with such sanctity of love ...
> Thou hast, Sebastian, done good feature shame.
> In nature there's no blemish but the mind:
> None can be call'd deform'd but the unkind.
>
> [1] *looked after*

Antonio is taken off to the cells.

The failed duel between Cesario and Sir Andrew is a masterpiece of comedy. However, duelling and street-fighting were very much a reality in Shakespeare's day, although they were frowned on by the law.

A couple of years before the first performances of *Twelfth Night*, the actor and playwright Ben Jonson, a friend of Shakespeare's, had fought a duel with another actor, Gabriel Spencer. The cause of the duel is unknown; it is likely that the volatile Jonson had been stung by Spencer's criticism of his current play, *Every Man In His Humour*. The duel, fought with rapiers, ended with Spencer's death.

Jonson escaped hanging through 'benefit of clergy': this was an old custom which meant that anyone who could recite a Latin verse from the Bible could claim to be a member of the clergy, and escape the death penalty for a first offence. All Jonson's possessions were confiscated by the Crown, and he was branded on the thumb to indicate that he had claimed benefit of clergy once: it could not be claimed a second time.

Jonson's career recovered, but was always turbulent, marked by arguments with his colleagues and continual falling in and out of favour with royal patrons. Unlike Shakespeare, he was intensely conscious of the importance of his achievements. In 1616 he published a complete collection of his works: this aroused a largely hostile reaction, as plays were not generally considered worth reading and studying in the way that essays or poetry were.

Jonson's publication of his plays set an important precedent. Five years after Shakespeare's death, two of his colleagues set about the task of creating a complete edition of Shakespeare's plays, including introductory material and an engraving of the author. The resulting book was published in 1623. Although some of Shakespeare's plays were published individually during his lifetime, this collected edition of 1623 contained many plays – including *Twelfth Night* – which would otherwise have been lost.

Sir Andrew on the warpath

Viola, who had feared her brother drowned in the shipwreck, muses over what has just happened. Although she does not know who the stranger was, or what he meant, she heard him mention her brother's name. Perhaps there is at least a chance that Sebastian is still alive?

> *Viola:* O if it prove,[1]
> Tempests are kind, and salt waves fresh in love!
>
> [1] *turns out to be true*

When Cesario has left, the verdict of Sir Toby and his companions is unanimous. As well as being a coward, the young man is disloyal and dishonest. He has refused to stand up for his friend, and has stolen his purse into the bargain.

Sir Andrew is so indignant that, with encouragement from Sir Toby, he decides to go after Cesario and beat him soundly. The others follow: the encounter is unlikely to come to much, predicts Sir Toby, but it should still be worth watching.

Sebastian is bewildered   IV, i

Olivia, keen as ever to see Cesario, has sent Feste out to find him. The clown bumps into Sebastian and, mistaking him for Cesario, tries to persuade him to come to Olivia's house. Irritated by his persistence, Sebastian pays the stranger to leave him alone.

At this point Sir Andrew marches in boldly, followed by his companions. He has caught up with the treacherous Cesario – or so he thinks – and strikes him without further ado.

This is too much for Sebastian, who is already exasperated by Feste's attentions. He administers a sound beating to the unfortunate Sir Andrew. Sir Toby joins in the fray, seizing Sebastian. The clown races off to tell Olivia about the commotion.

The aggrieved Sir Andrew, not expecting such a fierce reaction from Cesario, tries to comfort himself with the thought of taking legal action:

> *Sir Andrew:* Nay, let him alone, I'll go another way to work with him: I'll have an action of battery[1] against him, if there be any law in Illyria; though I struck him first, yet it's no matter for that.
>
> [1] *charge of assault*

The struggle between Sir Toby and Sebastian becomes more violent, and they both draw their swords.

Another surprise for Sebastian

Olivia, summoned by Feste, rushes onto the scene to see Sir Toby crossing swords with her beloved Cesario. She orders him out of her sight, furious that his disorderly, hot-tempered behaviour has come to this.

Sir Toby and his companions make a hasty exit. Olivia apologises profusely to Cesario and tenderly invites him into her house.

Sebastian has no idea who this beautiful, warm-hearted and affectionate stranger is; but he is happy to let events take their course. For her part, Olivia senses that Cesario's resistance to her is breaking down.

> *Sebastian:* Or[1] I am mad, or else this is a dream:
> Let fancy still my sense in Lethe steep;[2]
> If it be thus to dream, still let me sleep!
> *Olivia:* Nay, come, I prithee; would thou'dst be rul'd by me!
> *Sebastian:* Madam, I will.
> *Olivia:* O, say so, and so be!

> [1] *either*
> [2] *if this is insanity, let love keep my sanity submerged in oblivion for ever*

The two of them go, together, into Olivia's house.

Malvolio is tormented   IV, ii

Following Malvolio's bizarre behaviour, Olivia had instructed her uncle to take care of him. In fact, Sir Toby has imprisoned him in a darkened room, and he, Maria and Feste plan to vex him even further.

Maria provides a gown and a false beard for the fool, who is to play the part of a curate with the name of Sir Topas. In this guise, Feste addresses Malvolio.

Malvolio pleads with the curate to go to the Countess and get him released. He is not mad, he insists: but Sir Topas refuses to believe him, telling him that he is possessed by the devil and unable to reason.

Malvolio is not trapped in darkness, Sir Topas explains, but in ignorance. When Malvolio maintains that he is in his right mind, Sir Topas tests him:

Feste: What is the opinion of Pythagoras concerning wildfowl?

Malvolio: That the soul of our grandam[1] might haply inhabit a bird.

Feste: What think'st thou of his opinion?

Malvolio: I think nobly of the soul, and no way approve his opinion.

Feste: Fare thee well: remain thou still in darkness. Thou shalt hold th'opinion of Pythagoras ere I will allow of thy wits,[2] and fear to kill a woodcock lest thou dispossess the soul of thy grandam.

[1] *grandmother*
[2] *consider you sane*

Feste leaves Malvolio and joins the others. Sir Toby is enjoying the performance, but is reluctant to carry on with Malvolio's mistreatment; he is already in Olivia's bad books after crossing swords with Cesario.

The clown goes back to Malvolio and – no longer in the guise of Sir Topas – feigns amazement at finding him in such a state. Malvolio begs the clown for a lighted candle and a pen and paper, so that he can write a note to Olivia and be freed from his dismal prison.

Despite another appearance by Sir Topas, urging Feste not to talk to Malvolio, the fool agrees to help him out of his predicament.

> " ... *Malvolio's humiliation and imprisonment seem so out of proportion to his offence that they lend the comic sub-plot a vicious air that adds to our uneasy sense that the play's comedy is darker than it seems at first. This disturbing quality is subtly reinforced by the repeated motif of madness* ..."
>
> Charles Boyce, *Shakespeare A to Z*, 1990

Meanwhile, out in the sunshine ...   IV, iii

Sebastian is in Olivia's garden, still unable to believe his good fortune:

Sebastian: This is the air, that is the glorious sun,
This pearl she gave me, I do feel't, and see't,
And though 'tis wonder that enwraps me thus,
Yet 'tis not madness.

Not realising that his friend Antonio has been arrested, Sebastian wonders what has become of him. There was no sign of him at the Elephant inn, where they had arranged to meet. Sebastian would love to have his company now, so that they could talk over the strange and wonderful turn that events have taken.

He cannot account for the sudden appearance of this beautiful stranger who seems to be so devoted to him. He knows he is not mad or dreaming, and she too seems to be perfectly rational; if it were otherwise,

Sebastian: She could not sway her house, command her followers,
Take and give back affairs and their dispatch,
With such a smooth, discreet, and stable bearing
As I perceive she does.

Olivia comes out into the garden. She too is overjoyed at this change in circumstances: Cesario's feelings for her seem to have undergone a transformation, and her love for him is now returned.

Olivia is accompanied by a priest. She cannot forget the pain of Cesario's earlier rejection of her, and asks if he will agree to take part, here and now, in a ceremony of engagement:

> *Olivia:*   If you mean well,
> Now go with me, and with this holy man,
> Into the chantry by: [1] there before him,
> And underneath that consecrated roof,
> Plight me the full assurance of your faith,
> That my most jealous and too doubtful soul
> May live at peace.
>
> [1] *nearby chapel*

The betrothal can be kept a secret for the moment, says Olivia; when the time is right, they will hold a formal, public celebration of their marriage.

Sebastian accepts without hesitation, and the two of them follow the priest into the chapel.

A prisoner is brought before the Duke   V, i

Feste is on his way to see Olivia, carrying with him a note from the distraught Malvolio, who is still locked up in darkness.

Fabian is anxious to see the contents of the letter in case it incriminates him and his companions, but Feste refuses to hand it over. As they quarrel, Duke Orsino enters. Among his attendants is Viola, still in her male guise of Cesario.

Orsino has come to see Olivia in person, determined to overcome her continuing resistance to his love. With the help of a little gold, he persuades Feste to find Olivia and bring her out to meet him.

As Feste sets off, Antonio is dragged in by the officers who arrested him. Cesario recognises him as the man who intervened in his failed duel with Sir Andrew. He explains to Orsino that he has reason to be grateful to the prisoner, although he did not understand the stranger's rantings about friendship and money.

Orsino too recognises the prisoner, but from very different circumstances. Antonio has been his sworn enemy ever since playing a prominent part in a sea-battle against the Duke. Orsino is amazed that Antonio has dared to show his face in public anywhere near his court:

> *Duke:*   Notable pirate, thou salt-water thief,
> What foolish boldness brought thee to their mercies,
> Whom thou in terms so bloody and so dear [1]
> Hast made thine enemies?
>
> [1] *grievous*

In reply, Antonio turns accusingly to Cesario – still assuming him to be Sebastian – and once more proclaims him as a traitor and a thief:

> *Antonio:*   … That most ingrateful boy there by your side,
> From the rude sea's enrag'd and foamy mouth
> Did I redeem. A wrack past hope he was.
> His life I gave him, and did thereto add
> My love …

Olivia's secret is revealed

Orsino is puzzled. Antonio claims to have been looking after the young man for three months; but that is precisely the time that Cesario has been with Orsino, at his court. Before the Duke can pursue the matter any further, Olivia enters, and he instantly loses interest in everything else:

Duke: Here comes the Countess: now heaven walks on earth.

After greeting Orsino, Olivia notices that Cesario is still attending on him; the same Cesario, she assumes, who joined her so recently in their private engagement ceremony. She hints playfully at the secret shared by the two of them:

Olivia: Cesario, you do not keep promise with me.
Viola: Madam –
Duke: Gracious Olivia –
Olivia: What do you say, Cesario? Good my lord –
Viola: My lord would speak, my duty hushes me.
Olivia: If it be aught to the old tune, my lord,
It is as fat and fulsome[1] to mine ear
As howling after music.
Duke: Still so cruel?
Olivia: Still so constant, lord.

[1] *offensive and distasteful*

The constancy she has in mind is to Cesario, not Orsino.

The Duke is exasperated. Over and over again he has offered his undying devotion; what more can he do? He must please himself, says Olivia, having by now lost interest in him completely. Orsino's passion now starts to veer into violent anger. If he cannot have his beloved Olivia, he threatens, he is almost tempted to kill her.

The Duke then announces dramatically that Olivia's affection for his servant Cesario has not gone unnoticed. He loves the boy dearly, but in his jealous rage the Duke is prepared to take his life as revenge upon Olivia:

Duke: ... this your minion,[1] whom I know you love,
And whom, by heaven, I swear I tender dearly,
Him will I tear out of that cruel eye
Where he sits crowned in his master's spite.
Come boy, with me; my thoughts are ripe in mischief:
I'll sacrifice the lamb that I do love,
To spite a raven's heart within a dove.

[1] *darling*

He starts to lead Cesario off. To Olivia's horror, Cesario offers no resistance. In fact Viola is overjoyed to hear that Orsino is attracted to her, even in her male disguise, and does not take his threat seriously.

In desperation, Olivia calls for the priest who conducted the engagement ceremony; she refuses to keep their betrothal a secret any longer. The priest confirms to everyone present that she and Cesario are indeed engaged to be married.

Orsino is furious at Cesario's deception. For her part, Viola is thrown into total confusion.

In Shakespeare's time, 'cut in the head' was a common expression for drunkenness. In this scene, the metaphorical is transformed, painfully, into the literal.

A sorry end for Sir Toby

Sir Andrew rushes in, wounded, wretched and crying out for a surgeon. He and Sir Toby have attempted another attack on the youth they took to be the cowardly Cesario. He has turned out to be more spirited in his defence than they expected, and both have suffered painful wounds to the head. Sir Andrew is alarmed to see that Cesario, the very man he is anxious to avoid, is present:

> *Sir Andrew:* 'Od's lifelings, here he is! You broke my head for nothing; and that that I did, I was set on to do't by Sir Toby.

Cesario denies hurting Sir Andrew: as far as he remembers, all they did was cross swords timorously before their duel was interrupted.

Sir Toby staggers in. He too is cut across the head. He inquires about the surgeon, only to be told that the surgeon is as drunk as he is. Miserable, defeated, and in disgrace with his niece, he abandons his pretence of friendship with Sir Andrew:

> *Sir Andrew:* I'll help you, Sir Toby ...
> *Sir Toby:* Will you help? An ass-head, and a coxcomb,[1] and a knave, a thin-faced knave, a gull?[2]

> [1] *fool*
> [2] *dupe*

The two of them make an unhappy exit.

The confusion clears

Sebastian enters. He goes up to Olivia at once and apologises for having hurt Sir Toby; it was in self-defence, he assures her. He reminds her tenderly of the vows they secretly exchanged a short while ago. Olivia, confronted with this second Cesario, is speechless.

Sebastian turns to Antonio, delighted to see him again after their accidental separation. Then he comes face to face with his double, Cesario, and is stopped in his tracks:

> *Sebastian:* Do I stand there? I never had a brother;
> Nor can there be that deity in my nature
> Of here and everywhere. I had a sister,
> Whom the blind waves and surges have devour'd ...

Sebastian and Cesario question each other closely about their backgrounds and families, and, amid mounting excitement, the truth quickly emerges: both the twins have survived the shipwreck, and Cesario is none other than Viola in disguise.

"The appearance of Sebastian does not dispel the basic ambiguity of erotic situations in Illyria, but, on the contrary, seems to aggravate it even more. Who has been deceived? Olivia or Orsino? Who has been deluded by appearance?"

Jan Kott, *Shakespeare Our Contemporary*, 1965

Two pairs of lovers

Olivia is still speechless with emotion. Sebastian assures her that, although she was misled in falling in love with Cesario, events have seen to it that her wish is satisfied.

Duke Orsino turns to Viola. The tenderness and affection he has always felt for his 'boy' are now becoming clear to him:

Duke: If this be so, as yet the glass[1] seems true,
I shall have share in this most happy wreck.
Boy, thou hast said to me a thousand times
Thou never should'st love woman like to[2] me.

Viola: And all those sayings will I over-swear,
And all those swearings keep as true in soul
As doth that orbed continent the fire
That severs day from night.

Duke: Give me thy hand ...

[1] *illusion, mirror image*
[2] *as much as*

Orsino asks Viola to abandon her male disguise. Viola explains that her own clothes – those she was wearing when she was rescued from the shipwreck – are still with the sea-captain who saved her. He is currently in prison; the man at whose charge he is being held is Olivia's steward, Malvolio.

> *"Orsino and Olivia are saved from their foolish and dangerous preoccupation with themselves by the exchange of a false love for a true."*
>
> Alan Hobson, *Full Circle: Shakespeare and Moral Development*, 1972

Malvolio's letter finally arrives

Malvolio! Caught up in the drama of recent events, Olivia had completely forgotten about him. She now remembers that he had suffered a bizarre fit of madness, and asks after him.

At this point the clown wanders in. He is still carrying the note from Malvolio who, he assures Olivia, is still mad. He starts to read the letter in a deranged, incomprehensible voice; it is the only way to convey the words of a madman, he insists.

Olivia impatiently asks her attendant Fabian to read it. She is shocked at its contents:

> By the Lord, madam, you wrong me, and the world
> shall know it. Though you have put me into darkness,
> and given your drunken cousin rule over me, yet have
> I the benefit of my senses as well as your ladyship …
> I leave my duty a little unthought of, and speak out of
> my injury.

She orders Fabian to free Malvolio at once.

Olivia then turns to Duke Orsino and proposes that the two weddings – hers to Sebastian, and his to Viola – should be celebrated on the same day, at Olivia's house. The Duke agrees: he is happy to accept Olivia as his sister-in-law, and Viola as his wife.

Malvolio boils over

Malvolio, finally released from his sunless prison, makes an ill-tempered entrance. He confronts Olivia immediately, and accusingly shows her the love-letter which started off the humiliating series of events.

> *Malvolio:* Pray you, peruse that letter ...
> And tell me, in the modesty of honour,
> Why you have given me such clear lights[1] of favour,
> Bade me come smiling and cross-garter'd to you,
> To put on yellow stockings, and to frown
> Upon Sir Toby, and the lighter people ...
>
> [1] *signs*

Olivia is dismayed by the letter, realising at once that it is a forgery designed to trick Malvolio. She recognises the handwriting as Maria's, and reassures Malvolio that the culprits, when found, will be punished according to Malvolio's own wishes.

Fabian intervenes diplomatically at this point. In order to restore harmony to this meeting of fortunate lovers, he says, he will gladly confess everything. He and Sir Toby initiated the trick against Malvolio, he admits, while Maria's involvement was minimal. The deception has had an unexpected after-effect:

> *Fabian:*   ... myself and Toby
> Set this device against Malvolio here,
> Upon some stubborn and uncourteous parts
> We had conceiv'd against him.[1] Maria writ
> The letter, at Sir Toby's great importance,[2]
> In recompense whereof he hath married her.
>
> [1] *attitudes we imagined we saw in him*
> [2] *urging*

He hopes, in conclusion, that their foolishness will be laughed at and eventually forgotten.

Feste, less tactful than Fabian, reminds Malvolio of his earlier condemnation of fools. As far as he is concerned, Malvolio has been taught a lesson:

Feste: But do you remember, 'Madam, why laugh you at such a barren rascal, and[1] you smile not, he's gagged'? And thus the whirligig[2] of time brings in his revenges.

[1] *if*
[2] *spinning-top*

Malvolio, enraged that his humiliation might be regarded as justifiable revenge, storms out. Olivia, concerned as ever for his well-being, is sympathetic:

Malvolio: I'll be reveng'd on the whole pack of you!
Olivia: He hath been most notoriously abus'd.
Duke: Pursue him, and entreat him to a peace …

Fabian goes after Malvolio to try to pacify him and bring him back into the fold.

I'll be reveng'd on the whole pack of you!

In a way that Shakespeare could surely not have foreseen, the puritanical Malvolio *was* revenged on the disorderly revellers.

In 1642, nearly thirty years after Shakespeare's death, radical Puritans in the English Parliament ordered a temporary ban on the performance of stage-plays, which they had always distrusted. Civil war between Parliament and the Crown was looming and, as the parliamentary decree stated,

"Publike Sports doe not well agree with publike Calamities ..."

The Globe Theatre, where many of Shakespeare's plays had been performed, went out of business. It was destroyed two years later, and the site was used for housing. The ban on performances was later made permanent; it was not overturned until the Restoration of the monarchy in 1660.

The Duke foresees love, happiness and harmony …

Orsino realises that they still have not tracked down the sea-captain who rescued Viola. For the time being, then, she must remain as Cesario: but shortly she will be able to change both her clothes and her identity.

> Duke: When that is known, and golden time convents,[1]
> A solemn combination shall be made
> Of our dear souls. Meantime, sweet sister,
> We will not part from hence. Cesario, come;
> For so you shall be while you are a man;
> But when in other habits you are seen,
> Orsino's mistress, and his fancy's queen.[2]
>
> [1] *is ripe, is suitable*
> [2] *ruler of his affections*

The two loving couples depart, their restless journeys finally at an end.

… Feste takes a more philosophical view

The drama is over, and the fool is left alone on the stage. He makes no comment on the strange series of misunderstandings, coincidences, accidents and deceptions that has finally resolved itself. Instead, he sings a simple song of one man's unfortunate progress through life.

> When that I was and[1] a little tiny boy,
> With hey, ho, the wind and the rain …
>
> [1] *just*

Feste's song is a brief tale of drunkenness and wasted opportunity, the song of a man who suffers equally through his own folly and others' hostility, and who is eventually defeated by the sheer relentlessness of existence:

> ... But when I came to man's estate
>> With hey, ho, the wind and the rain,
> 'Gainst knaves and thieves men shut their gate,
>> For the rain it raineth every day.
>
> But when I came, alas, to wive,
>> With hey, ho, the wind and the rain,
> By swaggering[1] could I never thrive,
>> For the rain it raineth every day.
>
> [1] *bullying, quarrelling*

But this is just one possible life; the world is full of countless others, a few of which we have glimpsed in the play. All are subject to the same rain, the same unpredictable, fluid and universal forces of change.

Change may appear to be for the better or for the worse; but, as the play has shown, what we take as one may prove to be the opposite. Either way, change will happen, and will continue to happen. We may as well welcome it, and learn from it; it is part of the natural order, like the rain, and like the storm which delivered the lost twins to the shores of Illyria.

> *... For the rain it raineth every day.*
>
> *"But I say unto you, Love your enemies ... That ye may be the children of your Father which is in heaven: for he maketh his sun to rise on the evil and on the good, and sendeth rain on the just and on the unjust."*
>
> Sermon on the Mount, Gospel of St. Matthew, King James Bible, 1611

For a moment it seems that Feste's song is going to move from one man's life to the whole of human history, but he gives up as soon as he has started.

It's a long story, he seems to imply: in any case, like the play which has just finished, it all ends up where we are, here and now, in the real world.

> ... A great while ago the world begun,
>> With hey, ho, the wind and the rain,
> But that's all one, our play is done,
>> And we'll strive to please you every day.

———
———

Acknowledgements

The following publications have proved invaluable as sources of factual information and critical insight:

- Charles Boyce, *Shakespeare A to Z*, Roundtable Press, 1990

- David Daiches, *A Critical History of English Literature*, Secker and Warburg, 1960

- Bertrand Evans, *Shakespeare's Comedies*, Oxford University Press, 1960

- Alan Hobson, *Full Circle: Shakespeare and Moral Development*, Chatto & Windus, 1972

- Jan Kott, *Shakespeare Our Contemporary*, Doubleday, 1965

- Gary Taylor, *Reinventing Shakespeare*, Hogarth Press, 1990

- Peter Thomson, *Shakespeare's Professional Career*, Cambridge University Press, 1992

- Mark Van Doren, *Shakespeare*, Henry Holt, 1939

- John Wain, *The Living World of Shakespeare: A Playgoer's Guide*, Macmillan, 1964

- Stanley Wells, *Shakespeare: A Dramatic Life*, Sinclair-Stevenson, 1994

- John Dover Wilson, *Life in Shakespeare's England*, Cambridge University Press, 1911

All quotations from *Twelfth Night* are taken from the Arden edition.

Guides currently available in the *Shakespeare Handbooks* series are:

- ❑ **Antony & Cleopatra** (ISBN 978 1 899747 02 3, £4.95)

- ❑ **As You Like It** (ISBN 978 1 899747 00 9, £4.95)

- ❑ **Hamlet** (ISBN 978 1 899747 07 8, £4.95)

- ❑ **Henry IV, Part 1** (ISBN 978 1 899747 05 4, £4.95)

- ❑ **Julius Caesar** (ISBN 978 1 899747 11 5, £4.95)

- ❑ **King Lear** (ISBN 978 1 899747 03 0, £4.95)

- ❑ **Macbeth** (ISBN 978 1 899747 04 7, £4.95)

- ❑ **A Midsummer Night's Dream** (ISBN 978 1 899747 09 2, £4.95)

- ❑ **Romeo & Juliet** (ISBN 978 1 899747 10 8, £4.95)

- ❑ **The Tempest** (ISBN 978 1 899747 08 5, £4.95)

- ❑ **Twelfth Night** (ISBN 978 1 899747 01 6, £4.95)

www.shakespeare-handbooks.com

Prices correct at time of going to press. Whilst every effort is made to keep prices low, Upstart Crow Publications reserves the right to show new retail prices on covers which may differ from those previously advertised in the text or elsewhere.